Holiday and Seasonal
BORDER CLIPART

Holiday and Seasonal BORDER CLIP ART

PHIL
BRADBURY

1990
Teacher Ideas Press
A Division of
Libraries Unlimited, Inc.
Englewood, Colorado

All of the designs in *Holiday and Seasonal Border Clip Art* are original and have been created by the author. Any resemblance to any other illustration or design is purely coincidental.

Individual borders and clip art elements may be used by the original purchaser of this book without special permission or additional reproduction fees. You purchase such rights when you buy the book. However, this book may not be republished in whole, or in substantial part, nor may the individual borders or art be resyndicated in either printed or electronic form.

Many of the designs from this book will be available as computer clip art. Contact the publisher for availability and price.

TEACHER IDEAS PRESS
A Division of
Libraries Unlimited, Inc.
P.O. Box 3988
Englewood, CO 80155-3988

Library of Congress Cataloging-in-Publication Data

Bradbury, Phil, 1946-
    Holiday and seasonal border clip art / Phil Bradbury.
    xv, 103 p. 22x28 cm.
    ISBN 0-87287-831-7
    1. Libraries and publishing--Handbooks, manuals, etc. 2. Borders, Ornamental (Decorative arts) 3. Library publications. 4. Library exhibits. 5. Holidays in art. 6. Seasons in art. 7. Copy art.
    I. Title.
Z716.6.B735   1990
025.1'2--dc20   90-5636
                                                              CIP

For Rita O. Bradbury
A Mom For All Seasons

CONTENTS

ACKNOWLEDGMENTS ix

INTRODUCTION xi

Section 1 — SPRING 1

Section 2 — SUMMER 21

Section 3 — FALL 37

Section 4 — WINTER 53

Section 5 — MONTHS 83

INDEX 99

ACKNOWLEDGMENTS

I would like to offer a special thanks to the wizards at Adobe Systems, Inc., who wrote Adobe Illustrator 88™, the finest draw program I have ever used, and to the folks at Jasmine Technologies for the excellent InnerDrive and the diligence of their technical support staff.

Technical Notes

All of the designs contained in this book were created on a Macintosh II containing 5 megabytes of RAM and a Jasmine InnerDrive 45™. Monitor used was the standard Apple™ Color Monitor. The software used for the majority of the illustrations was Adobe Illustrator 88™ and Adobe Streamline™.

INTRODUCTION

Holiday and Seasonal Border Clip Art contains 98 pages of illustrations and borders for use in preparing artwork for a wide range of promotional materials, including bulletin boards, transparencies, posters, flyers, and more. Sixty-six of the designs are completely new and have been created solely for this volume, and thirty-two borders, first published in the book *Border Clip Art for Libraries*, have been adapted in this collection for use by a wider audience. Nearly all the border designs are 7" × 9" to provide 3/4" side and top margins and a 1-1/4" bottom margin when used at actual size on a standard 8-1/2" × 11" sheet. The extra space provided by the vertical margin will allow for insertion of headers or page numbers for multipage booklets.

To increase the utility of the art and make it easier to create customized layouts, the clip art pages feature enlargements, reductions, reverses, alterations, and "flopped" variations of the art spots used in the border designs.

The book is divided into five sections: Spring, Summer, Fall, Winter, and Months. Borders and illustrations within each section are, insofar as possible, in chronological order (the actual date of some holidays, such as Martin Luther King Jr. Day, changes from year to year).

The best way to use this book is to simply familiarize yourself with its contents. A working knowledge of the illustrations and borders will make planning your materials a much easier task. Often, the designs themselves will generate ideas for different holiday and seasonal activities and promotions. In addition, many of the designs can be used for other than seasonal projects and events. For example, a bulletin board (or booklist, flyer, etc.) on humor could use the "Ducks and Curtain" border with the caption "These Will Quack You Up!" The hourglass cut from the "New Year's Day" design is appropriate to illustrate any time-related theme such as "Time to ..." (think about college?, plan your vacation?, study?, etc.).

Techniques

The two principal printing methods the purchaser of this book is most likely to use are photocopying and photo-offset printing. Photocopying as a printing process has several advantages over photo-offset reproduction. The cost is generally lower, especially for short runs; editing and making changes is much easier; the time between concept and finished piece is certainly shorter; and there is a greater degree of control over the entire process. The disadvantages of using a photocopier instead of a printing press are lower technical quality; restrictions on the kind, size, and color of paper stock which can be used; and limitations on the use of colored inks.

If the illustrations are to be reproduced in a photocopier, be sure to apply a white opaque along the edges of pasted-up elements to avoid shadow lines. Another method of eliminating shadow lines (and a good idea for borders which are used often) is to have the border made into a transparency. Type your copy in position on a page, lay the transparency over the typed copy, and photocopy both at the same time.

The border designs will also work well when reproduced through the use of electronic stencils. To print a design in two colors in an electronic stencil machine, it is not necessary to make two artworks or to prepare an overlay. Simply make two stencils of the entire artwork. With cellophane tape mask out selected areas on each stencil (e.g., mask out the border on one and the headlines on the other). This will have the added benefit of making proper positioning easier when the second color is run.

All the illustrations in this book are "line art." They are composed solely of areas of black or white; there are no gray or middle tones such as you might see in a photographic print. If you look closely at what appears to be a gray tint, such as the diploma on the "Graduation Day" border, you will note that what your eye interprets as gray is actually a pattern of small black dots. The smaller and further apart the dots, the lighter the tint appears to be.

For the most part these tinted areas will have no bearing on your selection of a particular design; all will reproduce equally well for a wide range of printed materials. It is a good idea, however, to avoid illustrations with screened areas (as well as drawings with thin lines or much small detail) if you are creating art for a T-shirt or bookbag which will be reproduced by the silk-screen process.

By combining elements of several different borders or adding/removing items in an existing illustration, you can create a variety of specialized designs for particular applications. For example, the "In Case of Rain ..." design shown here uses the umbrella and raindrops from two pages in the Spring Section, combined with the drawing of a drummer from the Summer Section. Cut-and-paste and simple alteration of the hand shapes create a unique and appropriate design.

Resizing

The illustrations in this book have been produced in a variety of proportions and sizes, but you will undoubtedly find times when adjustment is necessary. When the proportion of the border is correct for your needs but the size is not, it is recommended that a photostat enlargement or reduction be made. It is a good idea when having a photostat made to fill the area inside the border that you plan to use with pieces of clip art, headlines, other small borders, and so forth. When you enlarge a border design, you are already paying for the "empty space" in the middle of the frame. You might as well put it to good use by having other art elements you might need enlarged along with your selected border.

When the proportions of a border need to be changed, i.e., the width or depth is not the correct size for the task at hand, it is often easiest to leave the corner elements in place and make changes by cutting through the sides of the border. Many of the designs use a straight line or a repeating pattern for their edges and can easily be adjusted in this manner. Simply position the corners and add or remove portions of the sides to achieve the size you need. When enlarging a design you may need to first make extra copies at original size to provide sufficient pieces of the line or pattern.

Signs, Posters, and
Bulletin Boards

Enlarging the borders for use on signs, posters, and bulletin boards can be done in several different ways:

Proportional Square Method—The proportional square method is a way for even the non-artistic to create well-drawn large-scale posters by literally dividing the drawing task into little blocks. It is the most basic and the most laborious means of enlarging an illustration.

A sheet of tracing paper or acetate paper ruled with proportionately larger squares (2" or 3") is also made. Simply copy the border or illustration square by square. When complete, rub the back of your enlarged drawing with a soft pencil (making it into a sheet of one-time carbon paper). Attach it, face up, to your poster board and go over the drawing with a sharp pencil or stylus to transfer it to your poster.

You can also lightly draw the enlarged squares directly on your posterboard and erase them after your drawing has been inked or painted. The advantage of using the tracing paper is that you then have an original on file and can quickly create additional posters if needed.

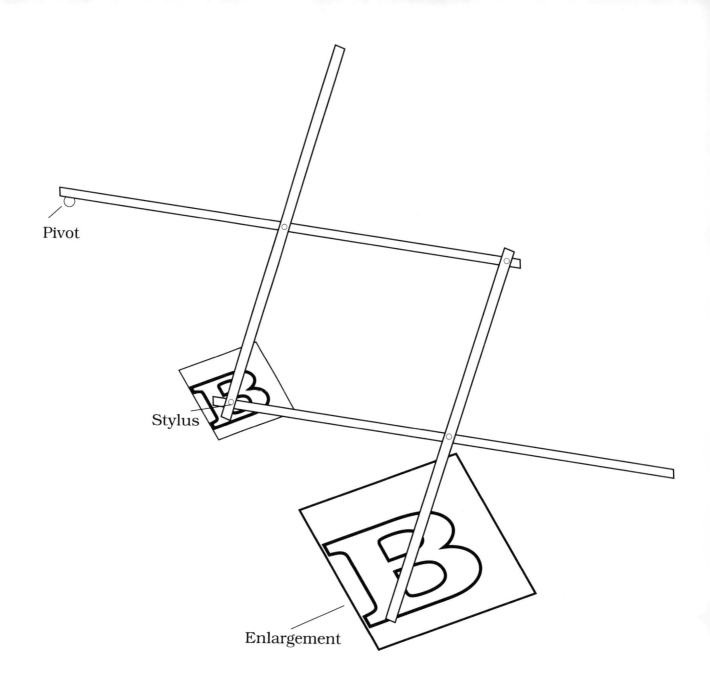

Pivot

Stylus

Enlargement

Pantograph—A pantograph will enable you to enlarge or reduce selected designs in precise size ratios. Once the device is adjusted for the desired size, simply trace the original with the stylus. An enlarged duplicate is produced automatically by a pencil lead set in the reproducing arm of the device.

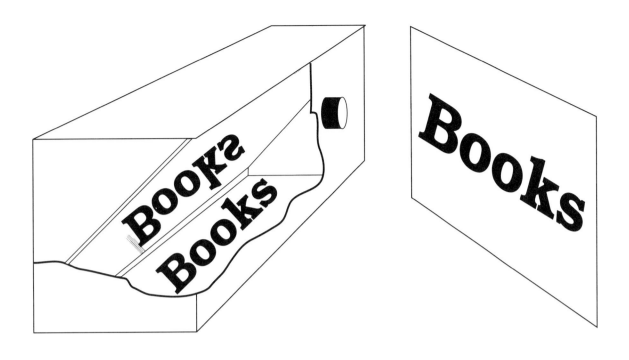

Opaque Projector—One of the fastest and easiest enlarging tools for poster, sign, and bulletin board work is the opaque projector. The material to be copied is placed within the opaque projector, and its image is projected onto a poster board attached to a wall or placed on an easel. The image is lightly traced onto the poster with a soft pencil and inked or painted to complete the work. (Designs which have been made into transparencies can be enlarged in a similar manner with an overhead projector.)

Photostats—While easily done, poster size photostats are expensive and have other drawbacks as well. Your enlargement will be on photostat paper; other items such as lettering and additional illustration must be done on the stat paper. The photostat will then have to be mounted on stiff backing board for display. Dry-mount presses which use heat are not recommended as they will often cause the photostat to bubble and discolor. Stat cameras work in black and white. If you wish to have your poster border in a color other than black, another enlarging method may be best.

Finally, while it is not necessary to be an expert in the graphic arts to use this book effectively—indeed, in large part *Holiday and Seasonal Border Clip Art* is designed expressly for use by people who are not professional graphic artists—a familiarity with the basic tools and techniques of the field will be most helpful in planning and producing promotional materials. There are many excellent books available. Two we recommend are *ClipArt & Dynamic Designs for Libraries & Media Centers: Volume 1: Books and Basics* and *Volume 2: Computers and Audiovisual* (Englewood, Colo.: Libraries Unlimited, 1988) by Judy Gay Matthews, Michael Mancarella, and Shirley Lambert.

Author's Note: If there are any designs or illustrations which you would find useful in your work but that are not in this book, please let us know so that we may include them in future collections. Please send your ideas and suggestions to: Phil Bradbury, RD 1, Box 219, New Albany, PA 18833.

Section 1
Spring

Spring! Spring! Spring!

March • April • May

March • April • May

Spring! Spring! Spring!

Applause!

Applause!

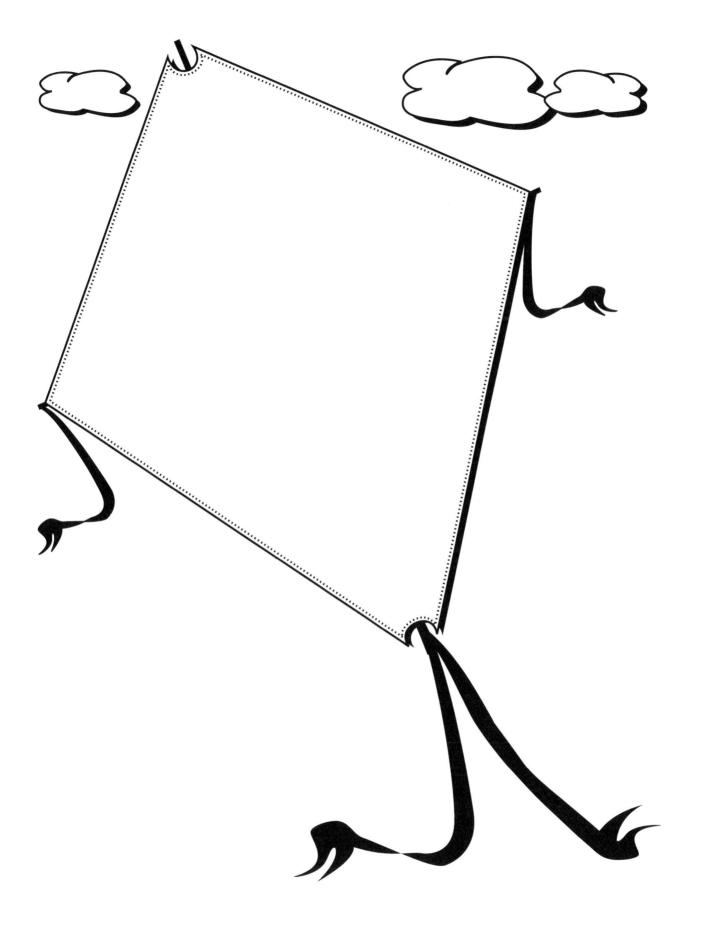

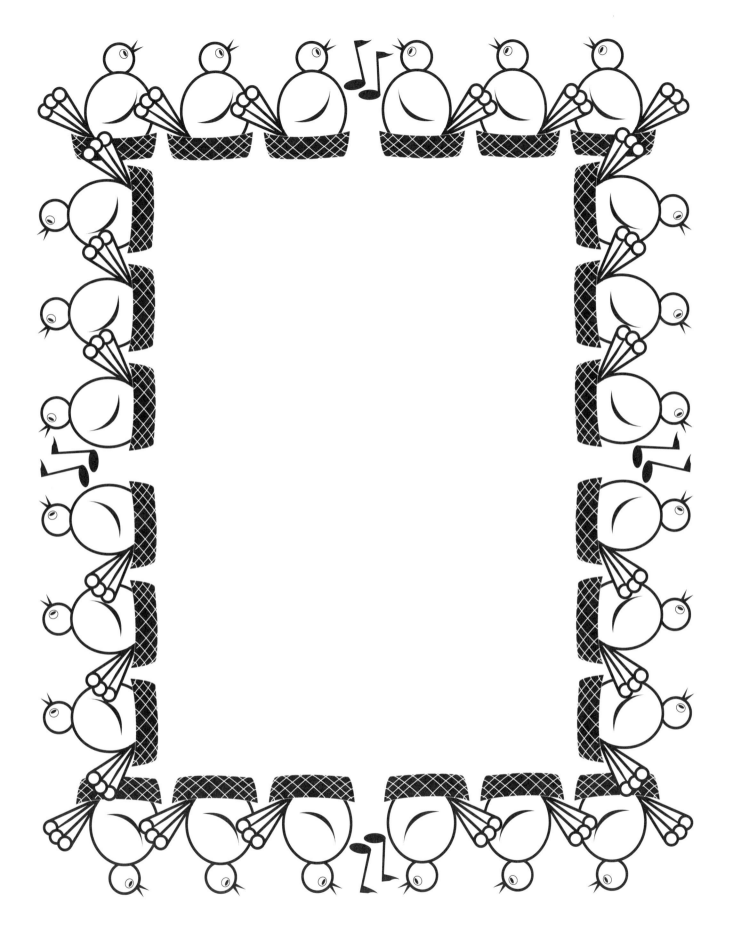

St. Patrick's Day

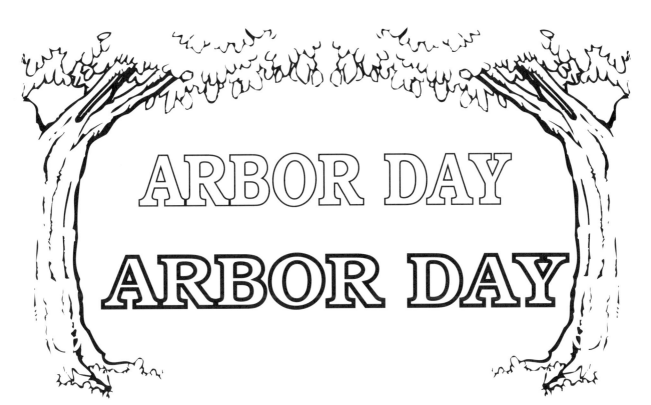

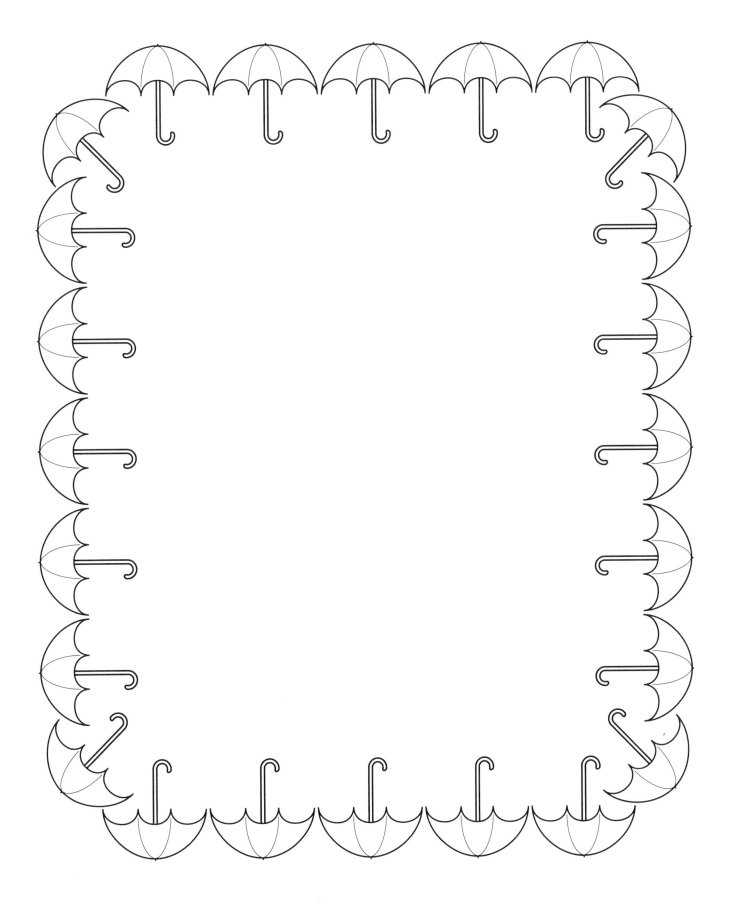

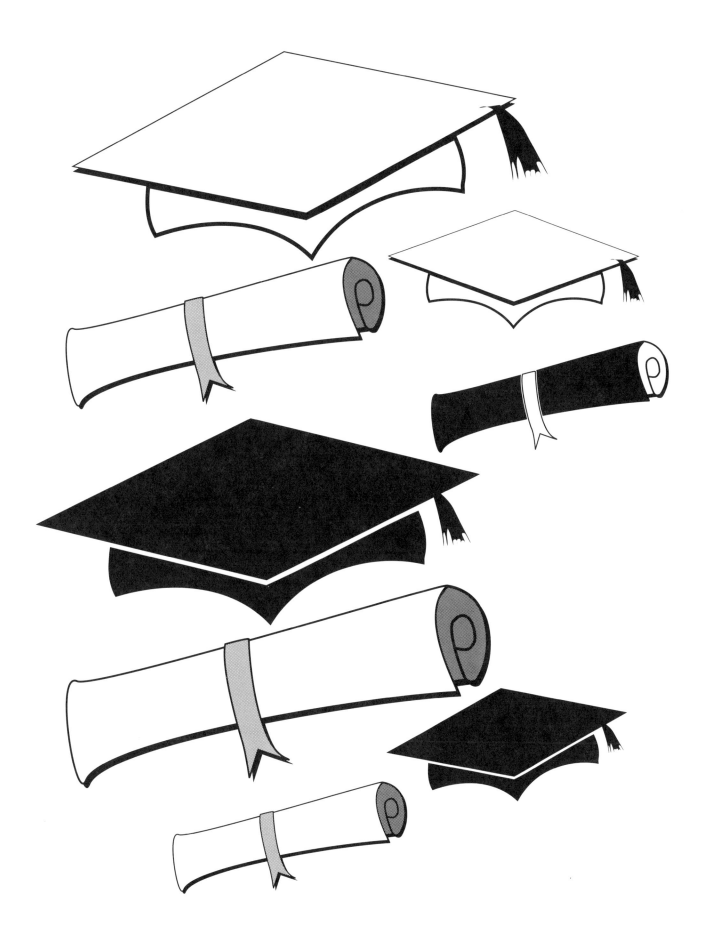

Graduation Day

Graduation Day

Flag Day
Memorial Day

Section 2
Summer

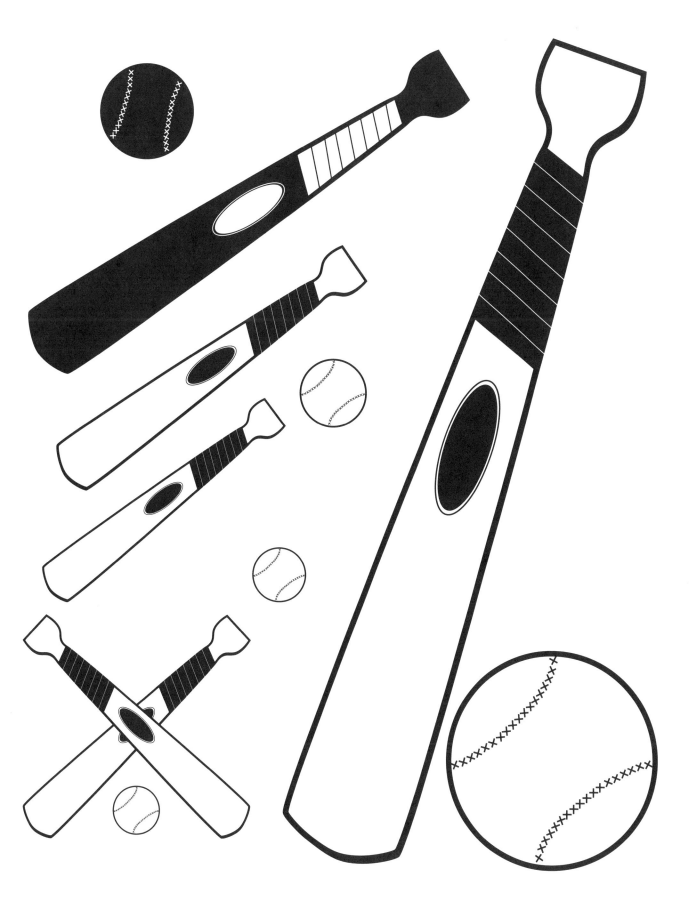

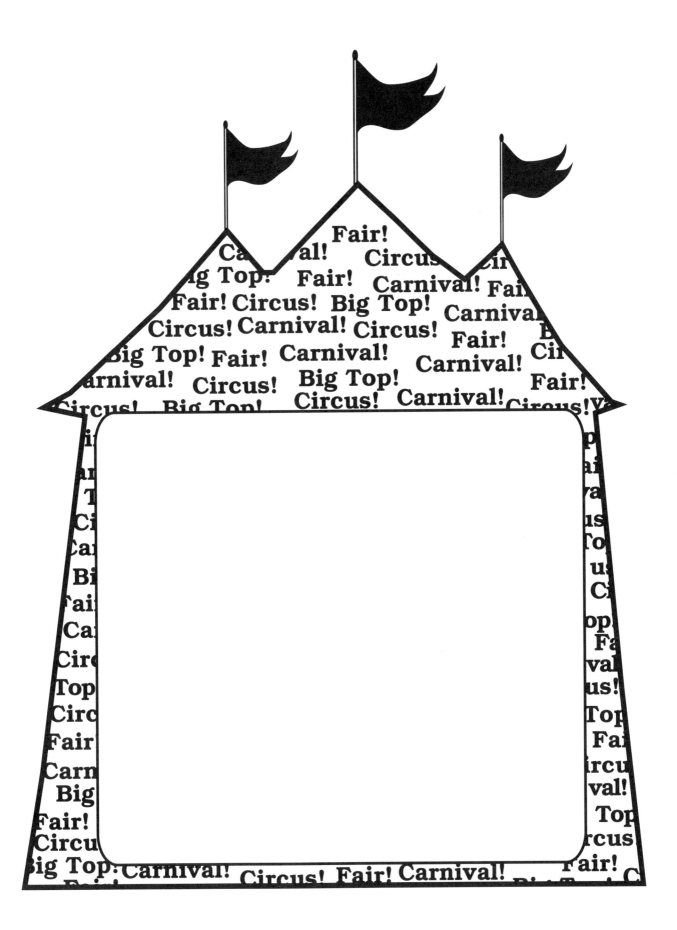

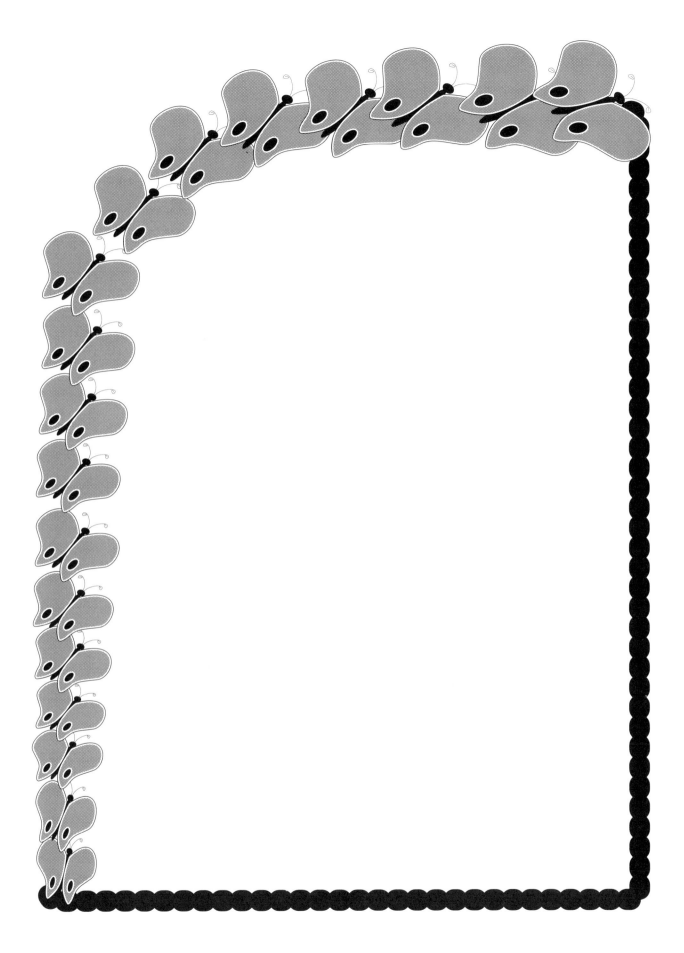

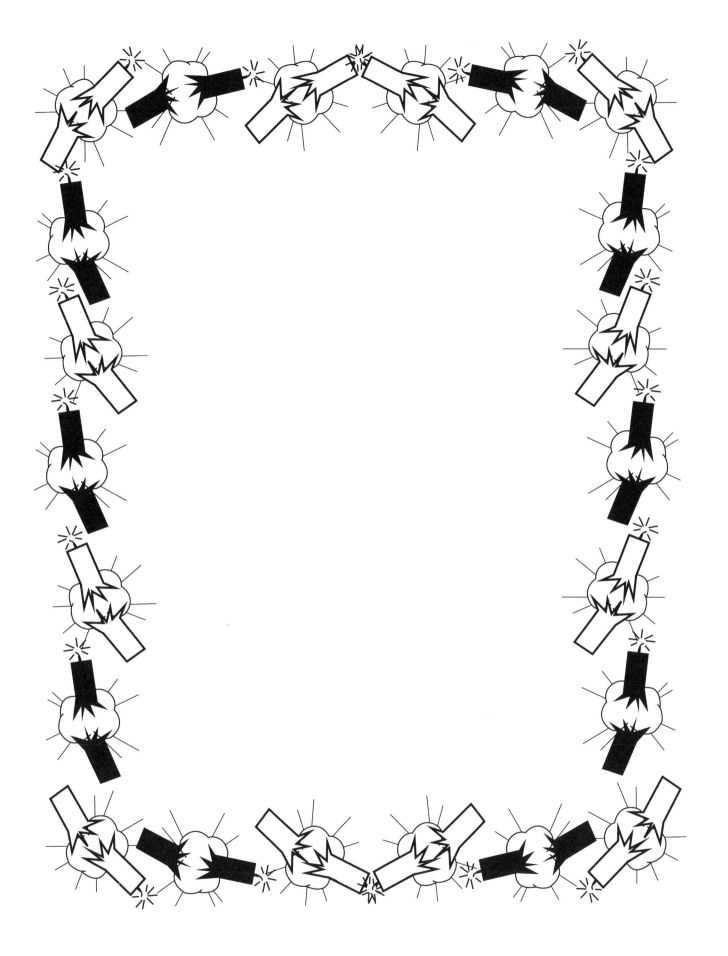

34

LET FREEDOM RING!
LIBERTY BELL

Section 3
Fall

FALL

September
October
November

September
October
November

School Days

45

Newspaper Week

Remove picture panel or "copy lines" as needed.

Section 4
Winter

WINTER
PROGRAMS

WINTER
PROGRAMS

Happy Chanukah!

—

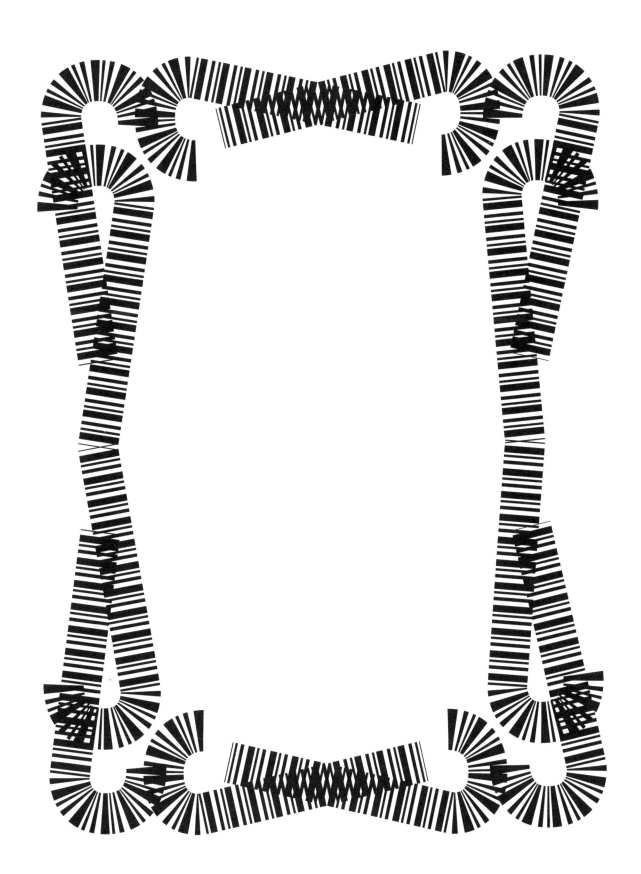

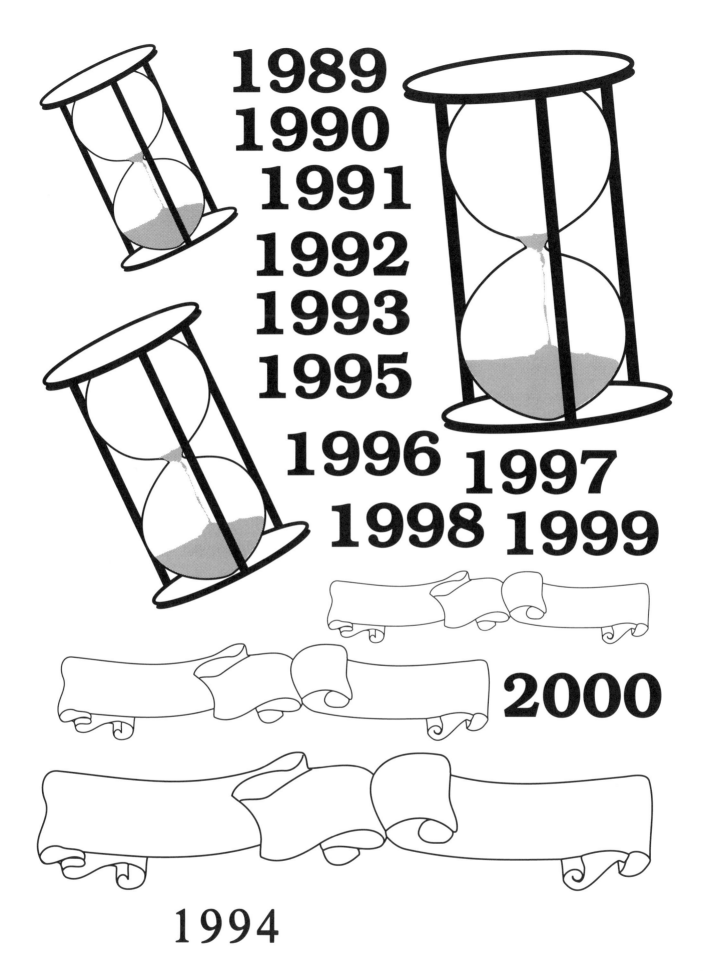

1989
1990
1991
1992
1993
1995
1996 1997
1998 1999

2000

1994

MARTIN LUTHER KING, JR.
1929-1968

**MARTIN LUTHER KING, JR.
1929-1968**

"I Have A Dream…"

Martin Luther King Jr. Day — January

"I Have A Dream…"

Martin Luther King Jr. Day — January

"*I Have a Dream...*"

Martin Luther King Jr. Day — January

Valentine's Day!

Valentine's Day!

Valentine's Day!

Presidents Day

Presidents Day

Presidents Day

Presidents Day

Section 5
Months

January
February
March
April
May
June

July
August
September
October
November
December

January
February
March
April
May
June

July
August
September
October
November
December

January February **March**
April May **June**
July August **September**
October November **December**

January
February
March
April
May
June

July
August
September
October
November
December

January
February
March
April
May
June

July
August
September
October
November
December

JanuaryFebruary**March**
AprilMay**June**
JulyAugust**September**
OctoberNovember**December**

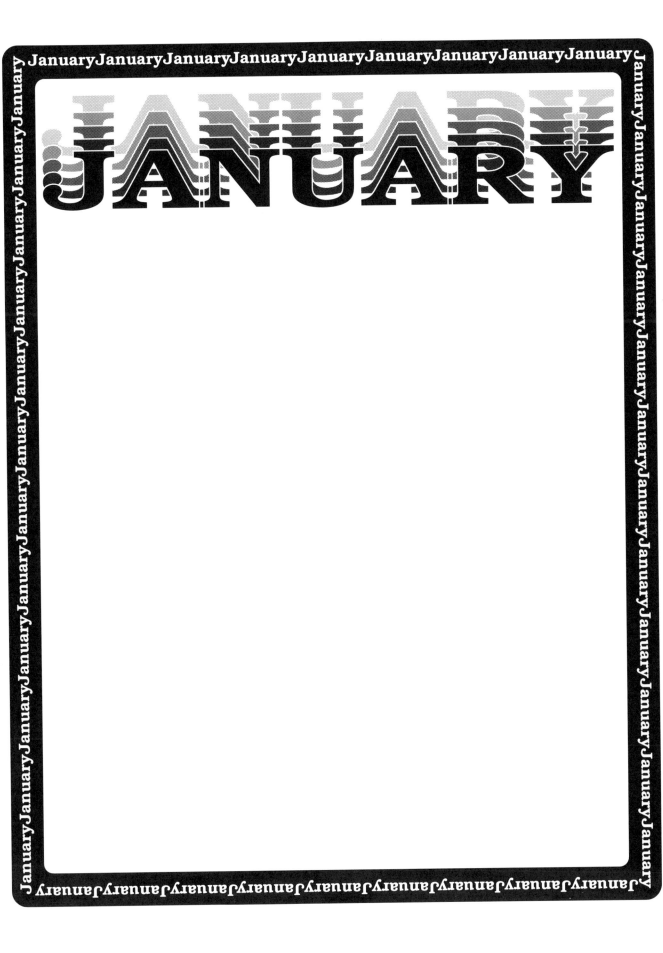

MARCH

APRIL

MAY

JUNE

JULY

AUGUST

OCTOBER

NOVEMBER

DECEMBER

Holiday Hours

Holiday Hours

INDEX

Abraham Lincoln, 78, 80, 82
Animals
  Bat, 45, 46
  Bear, 67
  Bird, 9, 10
  Butterfly, 29
  Duck, 4, 5
  Mouse, 65, 66
Applause, 4
April, 3, 83, 84, 85, 89
Arbor Day, 12
August, 22, 83, 84, 85, 93
Axe and cherries, 81, 82

Back to School, 40, 41
Banner, 71
Baseball, 23, 24
Baseball frame, 24
Bats, 45, 46
Bear, 67
Bears and candy canes, 67
Bells, 35, 69, 70
Big Top!, 28
Bird, 9, 10
Birds
  Duck, 4, 5
  Singing bird, 9, 10
Blackboard, 40, 41
Bunny, 14, 15
Butterflies, 29

Candy canes, 62, 63
Captions
  Applause, 4
  Arbor Day, 12

Back to School, 40, 41
Big Top, 28
Carnival, 28
Circus, 28
Fair, 28
Fall, 37, 39
Flag Day, 20
Ghost Stories, 47
Graduation Day, 19
Happy Chanukah, 59
Happy Easter, 14
Happy New Year, 72
"I Have a Dream...", 73, 74
Let Freedom Ring, 35
Liberty Bell, 35
Martin Luther King, Jr., 73
Martin Luther King, Jr. Day--January, 73, 74
Memorial Day, 20
Months, 83
Mother's Day, 17
Newspaper Week, 50
1989-2000, 71
Presidents Day, 82
Rain or Shine, 27
School Days, 42
Spring, 1, 3, 5
St. Patrick's Day, 11
Study Guides, 40
Summer, 21
Summer Programs, 22
Toys, 65
Valentine's Day, 75, 76
Winter, 53
Winter Programs, 55
Carnival!, 28
Chanukah, 58, 59, 68
Cherries, 81, 82

Christmas, 54, 60, 61, 62, 63, 65,
   66, 67, 68, 69, 70
Christmas trees, 54, 55
Christopher Columbus, 43, 44
Circus tent, 28
Circus!, 28
Cloud, 26

Daisies, 7, 8
Daisy frame, 8
December, 55, 83, 84, 85, 97
Drummer, 30, 32
Ducks, 4, 5

Easter, 14, 15
Egg with bunnies, 15

Faces
   Abraham Lincoln, 78, 80
   Bear, 67
   Bird, 9, 10
   Bunny, 14, 15
   Drummer, 30, 32
   Duck, 4, 5
   George Washington, 79, 80
   Ghost Stories, 47
   Martin Luther King, Jr., 73, 74
   Mouse, 65, 66
   Pumpkin, 48
   Smiling daisies, 2, 3
   Snowman, 54, 55, 57
   Sun, 21, 22, 26, 27
Fair!, 28
Fall, 37-52
   Back to School, 40, 41
   Bats, 45, 46
   Blackboard, 40, 41
   Fall, 39
   Ghost Stories, 47
   Halloween, 45, 46
   Leaves, 38, 39
   Leaves frame, 37

Newspaper Week, 50
Pilgrim hat, 51
Pumpkin, 48, 51
School Days, 42
Ship frame, 44
Ship, 43, 44
Study Guides, 40
Thanksgiving, 49, 52
Witch, 45, 46
February, 55, 83, 84, 85, 87
Firecracker frame, 33
Firecrackers, 33, 34
Flag Day, 20
Flags, 20, 28
Flowers
   Daisies, 7, 8
   Ring of daisies, 1
   Smiling daisies, 2, 3
Fourth of July, 31, 32, 33, 34, 35, 36
Frames
   April, 3, 89
   August, 22, 93
   Back to School, 41
   Baseball, 24
   Bears and candy canes, 67
   Bells, 70
   Butterflies, 29
   Candy canes, 63
   Circus, 28
   Daisies, 8
   December, 55, 97
   Drummers, 32
   Easter, 15
   Fall, 39
   February, 55, 87
   Firecrackers, 33
   Flag Day, 20
   Ghost Stories, 47
   Gifts, 68
   Graduation Day, 19
   Halloween, 46
   Happy New Year!, 72
   Happy Chanukah!, 59
   Hearts, 77
   Holiday Hours, 98

Frames (*continued*)
 Holly leaves, 64
 "I Have a Dream...", 74
 Ice cream cones, 25
 January, 55, 86
 July, 22, 92
 June, 22, 91
 Kite, 6
 Let Freedom Ring!, 35
 Liberty bell, 35
 March, 3, 88
 Martin Luther King, Jr., 74
 May, 3, 90
 Memorial Day, 20
 Mother's Day, 17
 Newspaper Week, 50
 November, 39, 96
 October, 39, 95
 Presidents Day, 80, 82
 Rain or Shine!, 27
 Santa Claus, 61
 School Days, 42
 September, 39, 94
 Ships, 44
 Singing birds, 10
 Snowflakes, 56
 Snowmen, 57
 Spring!, 3, 5
 St. Patrick's Day, 11
 Stars and stripes, 36
 Summer Programs, 22
 Suns frame, 21
 Thanksgiving, 49, 52
 Toys, 66
 Trees, 13
 Umbrellas, 16
 Valentine's Day, 76, 77
 Winter Programs, 55

George Washington, 79, 80
Ghost Stories, 47
Gifts, 68
Graduation, 18
Graduation Day, 19

Halloween, 45, 46, 47, 48, 49
Happy Chanukah!, 59
Happy Easter!, 14
Happy New Year!, 72
Hats, 49, 51, 52, 54, 55, 57, 60, 61,
 81, 82
Hearts, 75, 76, 77
Holiday Hours, 98
Holidays
 Arbor Day, 12
 Chanukah, 58, 59, 68
 Christmas, 54, 60, 61, 62, 63, 65, 66,
  67, 68, 69, 70
 Easter, 14
 Flag Day, 20
 Fourth of July, 31, 32, 33, 34, 35, 36
 Graduation Day, 19
 Halloween, 45, 46, 47, 48, 49
 Martin Luther King, Jr. Day, 73, 74
 Memorial Day, 20
 Mother's Day, 17
 New Year's Day, 71, 72
 Presidents Day, 78, 79, 80, 81, 82
 Thanksgiving, 51, 52
 Valentine's Day, 75, 76, 77
Holly leaves, 62, 64
Hourglass, 71

"I Have a Dream...", 73, 74
Ice cream cone, 25

January, 55, 83, 84, 85, 86
July, 22, 83, 84, 85, 92
June, 22, 83, 84, 85, 91

Kite, 6

Leaves, 37, 38, 39, 62, 64
Let Freedom Ring!, 35
Liberty bell, 35

March, 3, 83, 84, 85, 88
Martin Luther King, Jr., 73, 74
Martin Luther King, Jr. Day, 73, 74
May, 3, 83, 84, 85, 90
Memorial Day, 20
Months, 83-98
  April, 3, 83, 84, 85, 89
  August, 22, 83, 84, 85, 93
  December, 55, 83, 84, 85, 97
  February, 55, 83, 84, 85, 87
  January, 55, 83, 84, 85, 86
  July, 22, 83, 84, 85, 92
  June, 22, 83, 84, 85, 91
  March, 3, 83, 84, 85, 88
  May, 3, 83, 84, 85, 90
  November, 39, 83, 84, 85, 96
  October, 39, 83, 84, 85, 95
  September, 39, 83, 84, 85, 94
Mother's Day, 17
Mouse, 65, 66
Music, 9, 10

Nature
  Arbor Day, 12
  Bunny, 14, 15
  Cherries, 81, 82
  Ducks, 4, 5
  Flowers, 1, 2, 3, 7, 8
  Leaves, 37, 38, 39, 62, 64
  Singing bird, 9, 10
  Snowflakes, 53, 54, 56
  Stars, 31, 32, 36, 80
  Sun, 21, 22, 26, 27
  Tree, 12, 13, 54, 55
  Weather, 16, 26, 27
New Year dates, 71
New Year's Day, 71, 72
Newspaper Week, 50
November, 39, 83, 84, 85, 96

October, 39, 83, 84, 85, 95
Olive branch, 58, 59

Pilgrim hat, 51
Presidents Day, 78, 79, 80, 81, 82
Pumpkin, 48, 51

Rabbit. *See* Bunny.
Rain or Shine!, 27
Raindrop, 26,
Ring of daisies, 1

Santa Claus, 60, 61
School, 40, 41, 42
School Days, 42
School, 40, 41, 42
September, 39, 83, 84, 85, 94
Ship, 43, 44
Ship frame, 44
Singing bird, 9, 10
Singing bird frame, 10
Smiling daisies, 2, 3
Smiling flower, 2
Snowflakes, 53, 54, 56
Snowflakes frame, 56
Snowman, 54, 55, 57
Snowman skiing, 54, 55
Sports, baseball, 23, 24
Spring, 1-20
  Applause, 4
  Arbor Day, 12
  Daisy frame, 8
  Easter, 15
  Egg with bunnies, 15
  Flag Day, 20
  Flowers, 1, 7, 8
  Graduation, 18
  Graduation Day, 19
  Happy Easter!, 14
  Kite, 6
  Memorial Day, 20
  Mother's Day, 17
  Singing bird frame, 10
  Singing bird, 9
  Smiling flower, 2

Spring (*continued*)
  Spring frame, 3
  Spring!, 5
  St. Patrick's Day, 11
  Tree, 13
  Umbrella, 16
St. Patrick's Day, 11
Star of David, 58, 59
Stars, 31, 32, 36, 80
Stars and stripes, 36
Stars and stripes frame, 36
Study Guides, 40
Summer, 21-36
  Baseball frame, 24
  Baseball, 23
  Big Top!, 28
  Butterfly, 29
  Carnival!, 28
  Circus tent, 28
  Circus!, 28
  Cloud, 26
  Drummer, 30, 32
  Fair!, 28
  Firecracker frame, 33
  Firecrackers, 33, 34
  Ice cream cone, 25
  Let Freedom Ring!, 35
  Liberty bell, 35
  Rain or Shine!, 27
  Raindrop, 26,
  Stars, 31, 32
  Stars and stripes frame, 36
  Summer Programs, 22
  Sun, 26
  Suns frame, 21
  Weather, 26
Summer Programs, 22
Sun, 21, 22, 26, 27

Thanksgiving, 49, 51, 52
Top hat, 81, 82
Toys, 65, 66
Tree, 12, 13, 54, 55

Umbrellas, 16

Valentine's Day, 75, 76, 77

Weather, 16, 26, 27
Winter Programs, 55
Witch, 45, 46
Winter, 53-82
  Abraham Lincoln, 78, 80, 82
  Axe and cherries, 81, 82
  Banner, 71
  Bears and candy canes, 67
  Bells, 69, 70
  Candy canes, 62, 63
  Christmas trees, 54, 55
  George Washington, 79, 80, 82
  Gifts, 68
  Happy New Year!, 72
  Happy Chanukah!, 59
  Hearts, 75, 76, 77
  Holly leaves, 62, 64
  Hourglass, 71
  "I Have a Dream...", 73, 74
  Martin Luther King, Jr., 73, 74
  New Year dates, 71
  Olive branch, 58, 59
  Presidents Day, 82
  Santa Claus, 60, 61
  Snowflakes, 54
  Snowflakes frame, 53, 56
  Snowmen skiing, 54, 55
  Snowmen, 54, 57
  Star of David, 58, 59
  Suns frame, 21
  Top hat, 81, 82
  Toys, 65, 66
  Valentine's Day!, 75, 76
  Winter Programs, 55